Water Works

by Jamie A. Schroeder

I need to know these words.

dam

drink

electricity

firefighters

machine

well

People use water every day.
People use water for many
things. People drink water.

▲ This girl drinks water every day.

People must drink water every day. People need water to live.

▲ People need more water when they exercise.

People use water to clean things.
People use water to clean
their houses.

▲ This person uses water
to clean the floor.

These firefighters use water to stop a fire. People need water if a fire starts.

▲ These firefighters fight a fire with water.

The water comes from rain.
Some water goes into rivers.
Some water goes into lakes.

▲ The rain helped fill this river.

Some towns store water.
Some workers built this dam.
The dam helps store the water.
Many towns use this water.

▲ This dam stores water.

Some water is in the ground.
People use machines to dig
a well.

ground   pipe

water

▲ This hole will be a well.

A well collects water. Then the water flows into a house.

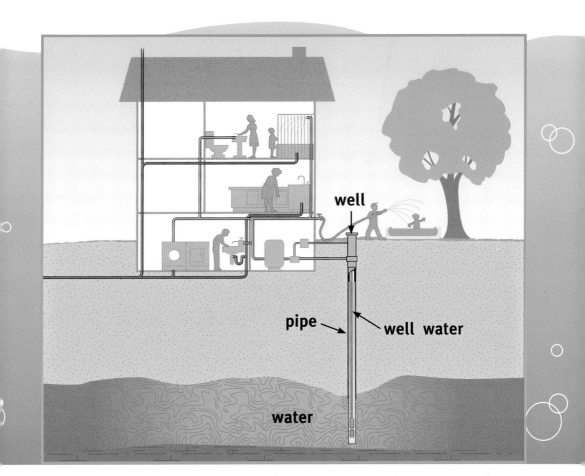

well

pipe → ← well water

water

▲ The water comes from under the ground.

People can use water to make energy. One type of energy is electricity.

▲ People will use this water to make electricity.

How can water make electricity?
First workers build a machine that
looks like a wheel. The water
moves the wheel.

▲ This machine needs water to work.

The water pushes the parts of the wheel. The wheel spins fast.

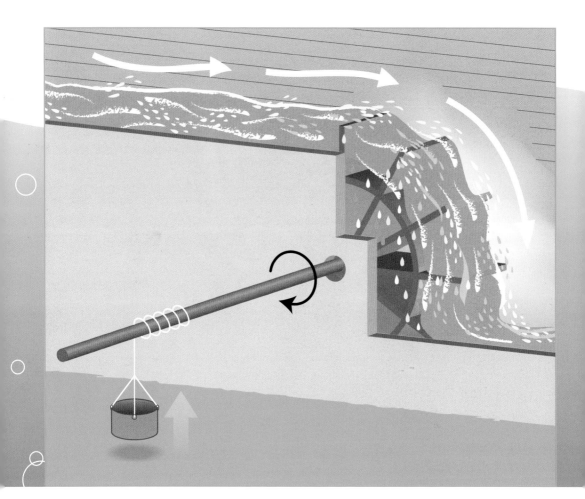

▲ The water can be powerful.

The wheel turns another machine.
The machine makes electricity.
People use electricity for light.

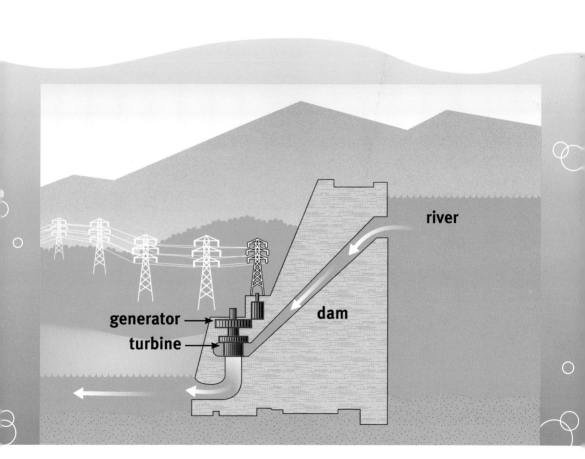

▲ This machine makes electricity.

People need water every day.
People drink water. People
use water to make electricity.
How will you use water today?